Eleanor Roosevelt
PROGRESSIVE REFORMER

BY CLARA MacCARALD

Published by The Child's World®
1980 Lookout Drive • Mankato, MN 56003-1705
800-599-READ • www.childsworld.com

Photographs ©: Katherine Young/Hulton Archive/Getty Images, cover, 1; Library of
Congress, 5; Everett Collection/Newscom, 6, 14, 17, 18; AP Images, 8, 10; WD/AP
Images, 12; Gerard Yvon Cheynet/AP Images, 20

ISBN 9781503823976
LCCN 2017944736

Printed in the United States of America
PA02362

ABOUT THE AUTHOR

Clara MacCarald is a freelance writer with a master's degree in biology. She
lives with her family in an off-grid house nestled in the forests of central
New York. When not parenting her daughter, she spends her time writing
nonfiction books for kids.

TABLE OF
CONTENTS

FAST FACTS

Full Name

- Anna Eleanor Roosevelt

Birthdate

- October 11, 1884, in New York City, New York

Husband

- President Franklin Delano Roosevelt

Children

- Anna, James, Franklin Jr. (lived less than a year), Elliott, Franklin Jr., and John

Years in White House

- 1933–1945

Accomplishments

- Wrote a daily newspaper column called "My Day" from 1935 to 1962.
- Held women-only press conferences, giving female reporters a chance to cover politics.

- Served as the first First Lady to host White House conferences, often dealing with the needs of women and people of color.
- Served as the first First Lady to have an official job while her husband was president.
- Worked to create and pass the **Universal Declaration** of Human Rights.

Chapter 1

FLYING HIGH

On an April night in 1933, First Lady Eleanor Roosevelt led family members and guests to a lit-up airport near the White House. Among her guests was Amelia Earhart, the famous female pilot. Although she still wore her evening dress, Eleanor was ready for excitement. The captain welcomed them into a plane the size of a bus. The plane soared into the air toward Baltimore, Maryland.

For part of the flight, Amelia took the controls while wearing white evening gloves. Eleanor did not want to be left out. While Eleanor was in the cockpit with the captain, the plane suddenly swung to the side. Amelia laughed. "Oh, Mrs. Roosevelt's flying the plane!"[1]

◀ Eleanor Roosevelt became First Lady on March 4, 1933.

▲ Franklin and Eleanor were married on March 17, 1905.

"It was lovely," Eleanor told reporters afterward. "It felt like being on top of the world!"[2]

Eleanor had a tough childhood. She lost both parents and a brother by the age of 10. She was a shy child.

Eleanor was then sent to a boarding school in London. Later she returned to New York. She worked to improve the lives of poor workers while dating her distant cousin, Franklin Roosevelt.

In 1905, Eleanor's uncle, President Theodore Roosevelt, led her down the aisle to marry Franklin. Together Franklin and Eleanor had six children. Eleanor worked at the American Red Cross and supported her husband's political career.

On March 4, 1933, Franklin became president of the United States. That night, Eleanor attended a ball wearing a long blue gown and a diamond necklace. Eleanor delighted in greeting the vast crowd.

Eleanor was the longest-serving First Lady. She also served as a new kind of First Lady, one who fought for important causes while maintaining an active social life. Sometimes she supported her husband's actions. Other times she opposed them. But Eleanor never stopped trying to improve people's lives.

Chapter 2

SPEAKING TO THE PEOPLE

In March 1933, Eleanor drove to the outer edge of Washington, DC. She pulled up at a campsite. The men at the camp were World War I **veterans**. They wanted money they had been promised by Congress for serving in the war. The payment had been put off for many years. Millions of people had no work because of the **Great Depression**. Eleanor was there to help.

Eleanor walked through thick mud to a line of veterans waiting for food. She felt uncertain how she would be received. Surprised to see her, the men invited her to join them in the eating hall. Eleanor was struck by the neatness of the camp and by the men's enthusiasm.

◀ Eleanor visited many camps during the 1930s, including Fort Hunt, Virginia, on May 16, 1933.

▲ One of the causes Eleanor championed was helping provide public housing for people in New York in 1935.

They talked about the war together. "I shall always be grateful to those who served their country," she told them.[3] The veterans cheered her words and sang songs for her.

The veterans followed Eleanor to her car. She wished them luck as they waved and sang to her. They felt the First Lady cared about them and their problems. Although they did not get their money right away, many would later join a program started by Franklin to provide millions of jobs.

Eleanor also pushed hard for women to be equal to men. Thanks to her efforts, thousands of women gained work, education, and experience at workers' camps. Eleanor often worked to advance equal rights and opportunities for women and people of color.

Eleanor reached out to the public as well. She gave speeches, wrote books and columns, spoke on the radio, appeared on film, and traveled to see how people lived. Many people reached back. They wrote her letters for help or advice. When people were in trouble, Eleanor tried to find organizations or government offices that could help them.

Chapter 3

A WARTIME FIRST LADY

E leanor made her way through the smoky **convention** hall in July 1940. The space roared with unhappy voices. The disorder worried Eleanor. Her husband was being **nominated** for a third term. His **political party**, the Democrats, were arguing over who would be Franklin's running mate. Eleanor was afraid the fierce fighting would tear the party apart.

Eleanor reached the front and stood in the glaring lights. As she spoke, the crowd fell silent. It was the first time a First Lady had given a convention speech. "We people in the United States have got to realize today that we face a grave and serious situation," she began.[4]

◄ Eleanor gave many speeches over the course of Franklin's presidential campaign.

World War II had seized hold of Europe, although the United States had yet to enter the fighting. She concluded that people must come together. They need to consider the good of the nation as a whole, not just their own interests.

No one spoke. Eleanor returned to her seat, unsure how they had taken her speech. The organ began to play "God Bless America." The hall roared with applause.

The Democratic party came together behind Franklin. He won the election. The next year, the United States entered World War II. Eleanor stayed busy visiting friendly countries and U.S. troops despite the dangers of traveling during war.

> "I personally want to continue to live in a country where I can think as I please, go to any church I please, or to none if that is my desire; say what I please, and within the limits of any free society, do what I please."[5]
>
> —*Eleanor Roosevelt*

▲ Eleanor helped bring awareness to many causes, sometimes over the radio.

Eleanor pushed for black troops to be treated fairly. One day in Alabama, she climbed into a plane behind a black pilot. She smiled broadly, hoping that one small act could strike a blow for **equality**.

Chapter 4

A DELEGATE FOR HUMAN RIGHTS

On April 12, 1945, Eleanor waited at the White House. She wore a black dress. She was terribly upset. She knew she had to stay calm for the sake of the country. Vice President Harry Truman entered the room.

Eleanor put her arm around his shoulders. "Harry, the president is dead."[6] Without warning, her husband had suddenly fainted and died earlier in the day.

Harry stared at her in shock. He would now be the president. After a moment of silence, he asked if he could do anything for her. "Is there anything we can do for you?" Eleanor replied. "For you are the one in trouble now."[7]

◀ Franklin and Eleanor were married for 40 years before he passed away.

▲ Eleanor gave many speeches about human rights throughout her lifetime.

Although she left the White House, Eleanor did not leave politics. Harry made her a **delegate** to the United Nations. One morning in December 1948, Eleanor listened as other delegates voted to approve the Universal Declaration of Human Rights. The declaration proclaimed human rights that everyone should have, such as the right to privacy and the right to be free.

Eleanor had written parts of the declaration. She fought hard for certain rights to be included.

Eleanor continued to be a champion for people until her death in 1962. She left the world forever changed.

"If we do not see that equal opportunity, equal justice and equal **treatment** are [granted] to every citizen, the very basis on which this country can hope to survive with liberty and justice for all will be wiped away."[8]

—*Eleanor Roosevelt*

THINK ABOUT IT

- Eleanor did many things as First Lady and after her husband died. What do you think people should remember most about her?
- Do you think other First Ladies have been inspired by Eleanor? In what ways?
- Some people thought Eleanor should run for public office herself. Do you think she should have? Why or why not?

GLOSSARY

convention (kun-VEN-shun): A convention is an event in which a group of people gather together. Eleanor was the first First Lady to speak at a major political convention.

declaration (dek-luh-RAY-shun): A declaration is an announcement. Eleanor helped create a declaration on human rights.

delegate (DEL-uh-gate): A delegate is someone who represents others in a meeting or group. Eleanor was a delegate for the United Nations.

equality (i-KWAH-li-tee): Equality is the state of everyone being treated the same. Eleanor pushed for equality for women.

Great Depression (GRAYT di-PRESH-un): The Great Depression was a time when the economy crashed beginning in 1929. Millions of people lacked work during the Great Depression.

nominated (NAH-muh-nay-tid): When someone is nominated, he or she is put forward as the best person for a job. Franklin was nominated for president four times.

political party (puh-LIT-i-kuhl PAHR-tee): A political party is a group of people who have the same opinions in politics. Franklin's political party was the Democrats.

treatment (TREET-munt): Treatment is the way in which something or someone is dealt with. Eleanor thought all people deserved equal treatment.

universal (you-nuh-VUR-sul): Universal means something is true for everyone. Eleanor helped the United Nations proclaim that certain human rights were universal.

veterans (VET-ur-uns): Veterans are people who have been in the military. Eleanor went to the camp to meet veterans.

SOURCE NOTES

1. Blanche Wiesen Cook. *Eleanor Roosevelt: Volume 2, The Defining Years, 1933–1938*. New York, NY: Penguin Books, 1999. Print. 50.

2. Ibid.

3. Ibid. 46.

4. Eleanor Roosevelt. "Address to the 1940 Democratic Convention." *Eleanor Roosevelt Papers Project*. Columbian College of Arts and Services, n.d. Web. 18 July 2017.

5. Eleanor Roosevelt. "My Day by Eleanor Roosevelt: July 4, 1940." *Eleanor Roosevelt Papers Project*. Columbian College of Arts and Services, 28 Apr. 2017. Web. 18 July 2017.

6. Hazel Rowley. *Franklin and Eleanor: An Extraordinary Marriage*. New York, NY: Picador, 2011. Print. 282–283.

7. Blanche Wiesen Cook. *Eleanor Roosevelt: Volume 3, The War Years and After, 1939–1962*. New York, NY: Viking Books, 2016. Print. 539.

8. Eleanor Roosevelt. "My Day by Eleanor Roosevelt: April 30, 1945." *Eleanor Roosevelt Papers Project*. Columbian College of Arts and Services, 30 June 2008. Web. 18 July 2017.

TO LEARN MORE

Books

Caldwell, Stella A., Clare Hibbert, Andrea Mills, and Rona Skene. *100 Women Who Made History: Remarkable Women Who Shaped Our World.* New York, NY: DK Publishing, 2017.

Mahaney, Ian F. *Franklin Delano Roosevelt.* Mankato, MN: The Child's World, 2017.

Pascal, Janet B. *What Was the Great Depression?* New York, NY: Grosset and Dunlap, 2015.

Web Sites

Visit our Web site for links about Eleanor Roosevelt: childsworld.com/links

Note to Parents, Teachers, and Librarians: We routinely verify our Web links to make sure they are safe and active sites. So encourage your readers to check them out!

INDEX